A*Preponderance* OF THOUGHTS

You may also be interested in the following Tamarind Hill Press titles:

The Illusions of Life by Antonio J. Erskine
Streams of Pasion by Soji
A Sinner's Insanity Prolonged by Chenson A. Bennett
Consciously 21 by Saun-Jaye Brown
The Power of True Forgiveness by Suzette-Grant Walker

To find out where to purchase these and other THP books, visit www.tamarindhillpress.co.uk

Wholesalers can contact us on
info@tamarindhillpress.co.uk

A Preponderance
OF THOUGHTS

A COLLECTION OF POEMS

Ceyleena J. Green

Reviews

"This is truly an eye opening and sublimely honest read, where the author unabashedly bares her tortured soul. Reflections of hope, contemplation of suicide, the love for her child, and the rawness of her internalized anguish are all nakedly strung together in such a beautiful manner. Each poem will place the reader firmly in her shoes as they set upon the journey of hopelessness to resounding triumph."
– Ritchie Drenz, Author

"This book certainly belongs on my night stand and yours too. A Preponderance of Thought is meant to feed your mind and it surely did that for me. It has all the wisdom, upliftment, and encouragement that women need, both young and old. It will be a great gift to yourself. I can't wait to read more works from this author."
– Saun-Jaye Brown, Poet and Author

"Each reader will be captivated and connected by this book be it experiences, culture, perspective, gender or general issues faced in life."
– Marvyn Murdoch, Poet and Author

Table of Contents

For my daughter and my dad...

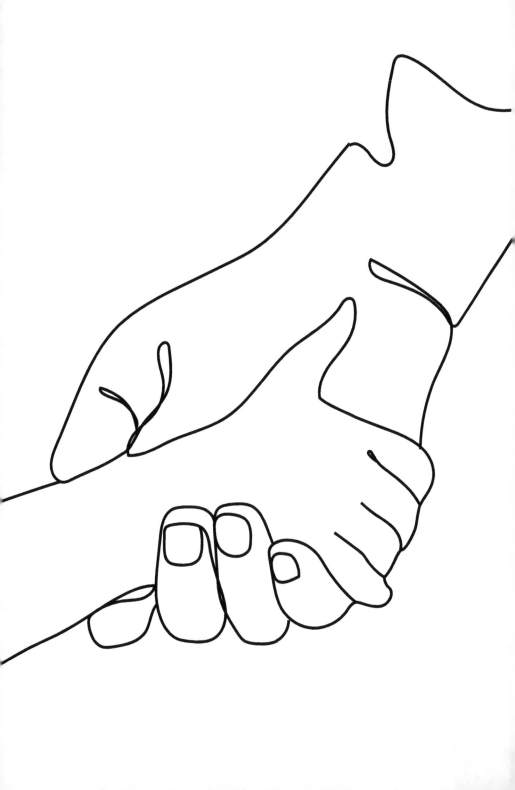

Preface

It is said that when all you see is darkness, you must look within for that beacon of light to guide you back to where you ought to be.

A couple of years ago, I had a bout of depression that was so severe that I contemplated suicide.

It was during this darkness and uncertainty that I wrote this book. I had to write myself out of a soul-wrenching depression and these poems literally saved my life.

As I penned each poem, my fears, anxiety, pain, hurt, and despair went, and I slowly began my road to recovery. I found myself with every stroke of the pen, and in essence, I became my own saviour. New life began to bloom, and slowly, I got back on my feet.

This book represents every random thought, every emotion felt, and every word spoken during that spiralling darkness, a darkness I overcame because of the grace of God.

I found my true self and the author and poet in me was awakened. I became alive again.

Writing saved my life.

Acknowledgements

Firstly, let me begin by acknowledging the wind beneath my wings, the blessing that never ceases, my Lord and Saviour, Jesus Christ. Holy Father, thank you for blessing me with the gift of writing, for without you being the captain of this ship, none of this would be at all possible. Lord, you really are my source and my sustenance, and I give you praise because you are indeed worthy of it. Through it all, I have truly learnt to depend on and trust in you, Father. I thank you, Lord.

My beautiful inspiration, my love, and my motivation, my daughter, Amoya Lyn, in whom I am greatly pleased in all things and who always said, "You can do it, Mom. I believe in you." I love you, baby girl!

My father, Ronald Green, who always told me, "You are the most talented human being to ever walk the face of the earth. Now, believe it and you have already overcome the first obstacle." I love you, Dad.

And last but by no means least, my friends, who have always encouraged me to grow some backbone, and "just do it already." Thanks guys.

This one is for you all!

Dried Bones

"I speak life into these dried bones,
I declare prosperity and purpose in my soul.
My destiny will not be swept from beneath
these feet of mine
But will be revealed in the annals of time."

Ceyleena Green

Chapter One

Preponderance of Thought

I am sore tired of this nine to five,
This endless pursuit of trying to stay alive.
I look at my fingers and they are covered with blisters and corns,
A constant reminder that my hardships continue each morn.
I taste my sweat and its bittersweet:
It gives me hope of how good life should be,
Yet, reminds me of how hard it is to make two ends meet.
My back is broken, and my feet all bounded up,
Yet...still, I can't drink from the rich man's cup.
EVERY DAY, I work my fingers to the bone, to earn a life's pay,
While the rich man does nothing and still prospers and increases EACH DAY.
It isn't easy to see your dreams and goals die and go unfulfilled,
To watch the smile on your child's face grow cold and still,
To be just another unmentioned, unseen face of poverty,
To EVERY DAY wish to be someone else other than me.
I now grow older as my years are wasted,
As I try to fight to play this hand that I was dealt with.
God knows my struggles and He hears my cries and understands that life isn't fair,
So He gives me the strength to go on, as He wipes away my every tear.
Still, I'm sore tired of this nine to five,
Of this never-ending pursuit of trying to survive...

Introspective

One of these mornings, I'm gonna rise,
Swallow my insecurities and just fly,
Become who I was intended to be,
Spread my wings like a great eagle
And sail away to me.

One of these mornings, I'll forget all about my problems,
Wake up and open the door to a world of possibilities;
To emancipate myself from mental slavery,
To boldly go where I've never been before,
To find the meaning of my life at its purest core.

One of these days, I'm gonna wake up my own way,
Not too worried about the obstacles I will be faced with today,
Just doing what I do best...me,
Without any apologies.
I will be defiant, determined, and more dedicated.
At the request of my heart, I'll be less cowardly and more motivated.

One of these days, I'll stop and listen to the piper's song,
To determine if He is right and if I am wrong.
I'll make good on my bags of tricks that I've used to erode myself with,
I'll be that no holds barred, spitfire woman that I have lost to this world,
Then I'll bow my head, tip my hat, and do a whimsical twirl.

One of these days, I'll rise above my flaws,
To just be me without any rhyme, reason, or cause,
To embrace the truth about my identity,
Allow love to develop, grow, and envelope me.
I'll let it touch, massage, and caress these kinks
That hate and unforgiveness brings,
And then I'll truly let go of all my fears and trials,
So that I can see me through a fresh pair of eyes.

Precious

I long for a simpler time, the simpler things, and a simpler
life
For the days when my hair was loosened by the wind and
gently combed by the soft breeze
The days when I ran through tall straw grass barefooted
Unafraid and unaware of tomorrow
A time when nothing mattered but the moment in which I
stood.
A time when mothers were mothers, fathers had
substance, and God was feared
Oh, I miss those days
When tamarind and mangoes littered the ground in
abundance like grains of sand on the seashore
When the air was fresh and crisp and pure
When nothing at all mattered but the moment that we stood
Those days when love was freely given without a thought
or reason.
Those magical days when the world seemed small and its
people untainted
When the lignum vitae rose and blossomed in all its glorious
splendour
Like the pride that shun on our unaffected faces
Those days when our playful narrow-minded youthful
exuberance roamed unabated and defiant in spite of our
hardships
Oh, to smile a child's smile, to live a child's life again
To see what we were then, now
And now that I'm older, my thoughts often stray to those
days when I knew what it was like to truly be free.

Chicken Soup

You better know your value and your worth,
While you are still alive here on this earth.
It's easy for you to lose yourself and your sense of
identity,
As you allow yourself to fall victim to this life's hypocrisy.
You better find and pluck that weed of a root,
That compels you to embrace lies, as it strangles the truth.
Get comfortable in that beautiful skin you are in,
Allow yourself to be you, even when no one else is looking.

Try your utmost best at all times to listen to that calm,
assuring voice within your heart,
The one that seeks to build you up and not the one that
seeks to tear you apart.
Believe in you and who you aspire to be,
Cause no one else is quite like you, not him, not her, and
most definitely, not me.
Learn to love and accept yourself for who you really are,
The real you, with all your insecurities and flaws,
And even the you, who hide behind those scars.
Seek to pull from the good and never the bad experiences,
Get acquainted with your strengths while you improve upon
your weaknesses.
Grant yourself wishes, anything from the mundane to the
monumental,
Get back to the core of you, get back to the
fundamentals.

Consider your feelings as well as those of others,
But don't give in to the selfish and unreasonable requests
and demands of friends and lovers.
Assure yourself, rather, brace yourself because failures,
struggles, pain, and obstacles will undoubtedly come your
way and you most certainly will cry.
But remember the God in you and whose you are,
As you embark on your journey,
The journey to live...
 Before you die.

Hope Road

I sure wish I was rich
I would buy me a big ole house on the hill
Fix my life and my daughter's too
Throw out my old life and start anew

I would fix my hair so as to keep up with the Joneses
I would dig up my dandelions and plant me some roses
I would buy me a car even though I can't drive
Oh man, that would sure be the good life

I would go back to Church and live my life right
With no more problems, my life will sure be bright
I would give my baby girl everything she deserves
Give her all the love she needs without any of the hurts
I would marry me a man perfect and divine
And each day, we would both get drunk on life's wine

'Cause God knows my life has been no crystal stairs
It's been filled with so much brokenness and a whole lot of despair
And with only four pennies and a nickel to my name
Oh Lord, when I get rich, my life will never be the same.

My Words

MY words are too real to ever be thrown back in my face.

They are too powerful and mighty to ever be tampered with or erased.

MY words are like an old Negro spiritual that impregnates the thoughts and uplifts the consciousness of those around me.

THEY are like a shout to the ears, a shock to the heart, and nourishment for the spiritually poor and needy.

THEY transcend me and they define me.

THEY are who I am and who I will be.

MY words sing a black woman's song

Of my dreams, my pain, my loves, all day long.

THEY can tear down barriers, destroy fences, and eliminate walls.

THEY are sweet, loving, encouraging, tender, and kind.

THEY are like soul food for all mankind.

MY words aren't twisted, double fisted, or shifted.

No, MY words are far sleeker and meeker than that.

THEY are medicine for a diminishing race, salt for a tasteless and bland existence, the jalapenos for a dull and spice-less world.

Even so, MY words are more than you or I will ever know.

MY words are defiant like Malcolm X, as proud as Marcus Garvey, as charismatic as Martin Luther King, as phenomenal as Maya Angelou, as revolutionary as Bob Marley, and as infinite as Jesus Christ.

MY words are an ode to my past and a lamp and path to my future.
Even so, MY words are so much more than you or I will ever know.

Cathartic

Each day I rise with a prayer,
Thankful for another opportunity to right my wrongs,
To sing a black woman's song.
And even though my back is now pressed heavily against
life's wall,
I still push against the grain so that I will stand tall.

Each day I rise to be better than I was the day before,
To be wiser, more tolerant, less arrogant, cognizant of the
needs of the poor.
I'm more than this caramel coated skin that I'm in,
I'm a woman, a daughter, a sister, a mother, a lover, a
friend,
But most beautifully, a human being.

Each day I rise to overcome, to persevere, and to
actualize,
But each time I'm oppressed by your hypocrisy, your
apathy, and your lies.
You say I'm underprivileged and uneducated and don't
deserve to be here,
Too uncouth, too unrefined, too ghetto that's all you ever
convey with your hateful whispers and disdain-filled stares.

Each day I rise only to be ignored, misunderstood,
discriminated, hated, unappreciated, and rejected,
But still, I rise to a higher me that is being perfected.

Still, I rise to silence the hypocrites, the elitists, the classists, the naysayers, the critics, and the authors of lies.
Still, I rise to witness no real change or empathy in their eyes.
Still, I rise to stand tall off these bloodied bended knees.
Still, I rise to embrace myself and my authority.
Still, I rise to defy all odds to win.
Still, I rise to find my place in this world again.
Still, I rise more dedicated, determined, resilient, strong, proud, and Black.
Still, I rise with my dignity, morals, integrity, and my self-esteem intact,
And if that makes me flawed, then quite frankly, I'm alright with that.

Burgeoning

Petrified,
Was my state of mind.
As I tightly gripped the metal bars on my bed,
Fearful of the task ahead ,
The doctors commanded me to "Push."
My belly distended, suddenly reduced to a mere holding cell,
To a life desperately seeking freedom.
I screamed in pain,
Uttering, that this will never happen again,
But to what end?

Sweat dripped from my face,
As the warmth of the sun filled the room.
As you frantically tried to escape my womb,
My clutch became weakened.
As I pushed, your head emerged,
Reality had now set in, this was really happening,

Your shoulder emerged,
The doctor made a feverish pull
To release you from your cocoon.
You were born,
The sacrifice was made
I lied, relieved of the pain,
For now,
I am your mother.

Youth is fleeting,
Yet sacred.
It quantifies and guarantees true freedom.
It apologizes for our faults
As it glosses over our mistakes.
It is an entitlement,
That window of opportunity that closes very quickly.
It allows for a time of sweet happiness that cannot be
described,
That is untouched by fears.
It empowers us to do and want more,
It makes us vulnerable and aloof yet invincible.

Youth is not just a sense of time
But a catalyst for introspection and appreciation of
oneself and abilities.
It remains the one true agent against age
And defies it whilst it instils the importance of it,
Creating a seamless transition from angst and rebellion to
wisdom and understanding.

Youth can never be manufactured, bottled, or sold in jars,
For it is found in embracing and accepting the knowledge
that beauty will ultimately fade and the undeniable fact that
aging is inevitable.

Youth isn't an ornament to be worn loosely around one's
neck,

For it is more valuable than diamonds,
More precious than gems,
And far more exquisite than any pearl.
It is to be treasured and cherished by all,
But never worshipped.
For when it is no more,
All that will remain is either regrets or purpose of self.

Grey Hairs

I see her in me...
I see myself in her...
She sits unaffected as peace befalls her lovely face,
She smiles as she remembers those days,
She touches her face now draped in wisdom,
Her grey hairs gently caressing her cheeks
Where her first kiss still lingered.
Her smile tells a story of hardships and endurance,
Of the battles she had lost and the many wars she had
won,
Yet her humility remained constant.
Her proud stride now bent is an effect of the struggles
felt,
But through it all, her fight to overcome intensified.
Her heart is no longer guarded but open to all,
Her words are manna; tonic for the lives of others.
A jewel she is to me,
A virtuous woman indeed,
An undeniable Queen.

Chapter Two

There sits an antique chair in a house, up the stairs in an attic, covered in dust and aged in despair.
For the one who once sat on it no longer lives there,
She now resides in a place that is dark and cold,
Betrayed repeatedly by the lies she was told,
She now lies dead, killed by what she thought was love.
Though aware of the decision she was making,
She ignored all advice and committed the ultimate sacrifice,
Unable to come to terms with the truth,
She decided to take her own life,
Instead of confronting and plucking the deadly root.

Be careful whose car you get into,
Be careful of the choices you make and the promises you break,
For all that glitters is certainly not gold,
Rather, an evil that will unfold.

Now, there stands a shelf polished in regret and stained with tears,
For the one who once used it now quivers in fear,
Never loved, never held, he became a victim of his environment.
Unable to un-weave the series of events that was spun,
He now finds his life shattered in ruins and his troubles has just begun.
Unable to grasp the weight of his decision,
He absconded the crime scene, now he's on a mission.

A mission to find the pieces of his broken heart to mend,
But with the life he took, his is now rend.

Be careful whose car you get into,
Be careful of the choices you make and the steps you
take,
For all that glitters is certainly not gold,
Rather, an evil that is yet untold.

There rests a diamond ring buried in a drawer, drenched in
betrayal and seething in deceit,
Because its owner is now faced with her own mistakes
and surrounded by defeat.
Once vibrant and enviable and full of life,
She now sits and ponders in her darkened room, staring
through her window blinds.
Unwilling to venture out into the streets to face the disdain
glares,
She resigns herself to a self-imposed mental prison of
over two years,
Crippled by the shame and travesty that had befallen her
perfect family.
For, you see; the chair, the shelf, and the diamond ring all
reside in the same house,
All abandoned because of the atrocities handed out at the
hands of a very abusive spouse,
Who repeatedly molested a daughter he swore he loved,
whilst he abused a son who only desired his love.
She is now forced to see what kind of man her beloved
husband truly was,
The one that caused the death of her daughter and the
imprisonment of her son.

The one that caused him that day to pull the trigger of
that gun,
That ultimately exposed the pain that he had managed to
keep,
That also forced his father to an eternal sleep.
She now grapples with the choices she had made,
And how they have caused all her dreams and hope to
fade.
If only she hadn't gotten into his car that very fateful day,
For with that one decision, she and her children have
certainly paid.

Be careful whose car you get into,
Be careful of the choices you make and the decisions you
take,
For all that glitters is certainly not gold,
Rather, an evil that is yet to unfold.

Savages

So it begins.
The desecration and destruction of a generation,
Our children being forcefully separated from their
innocence, which is their birthright.
Secretly, we sacrifice our young and drink their blood,
then discard their naked corpses openly in the streets.
They yearn for light and safety, but instead, find our cruel
intentions in the darkened shadows.
They eat the bitter herbs of our decadence as we grow
fat from their sorrows.
Have we no heart for their tomorrow?
Lest we forget today's victims are tomorrow's
perpetrators and seekers of carnalities.
Who then shall put an utter end to our impartial, unbroken
cycles of atrocities?

Our depraved and wanton need for flesh is now being
satisfied by the babe on the breast.
Mothers selling their sons and daughters for a profit.
But what profiteth a child when they lose their souls?
Fathers lying with their sons and daughters,
Severing the trust God entrusted them with,
Creating vipers and broken souls.
Children scarred by lust inevitably become splintered like
glass and scattered like dust.
We try to sweep their pain under the rug,
But each day, the seams of our wickedness and
deceptions are unravelled with one tug.

Have we lost our humanity, our conscience, and all respect
for the plight of our children?
Have we become that dejected that we can't see past our
noses?
While innocent lives wilt and wither away like roses.

Our children desperately beckon to us, but instead, we
turn a blind eye,
So uncaring we have become that we would rather
embrace our own lies,
Helpless and hopeless, they succumb to their defeat.
How many lives will be destroyed before we ever decide
to get up from our seats?

And we wonder why brokenness is on the rise.
Because when we had the chance to help, we held our
breath and closed our eyes,
We grit our teeth in hopes that their hurt will disappear,
But when lives are fractured in this way, it will take
forever to repair.

It isn't fair, to be born only to be abused,
To have your innocence stolen and used,
To feel your essence slowly die within,
To watch an innocent child crying in pain,
Knowing for them, life will never be the same again.

Who gives us the right to torture, mangle, and maim their
trust?
To take away that which is sacred, holy, and pure,
To exile our children to an existence of self-deprecation
of their core.

My people, until we agree that one innocence stolen is one too much,

Until we can relate and be open to the truth of the many lives that are being adversely affected by one deliberate sadistic touch,

Until we can say enough is enough, and mean it, and have open forums to decide,

And until the gap between justice for the abused and punishment for their abusers is narrowed from wide,

Until then,

My people,

We will forever be responsible for this generation's genocide.

Misery

What is this empty feeling I feel?
Is it that my God has abandoned me?
Has He spat in my face and ignored my pleas?
Has He dismantled my pride and brushed my needs aside?
Leaving me feeling so empty and lonely inside.
What have I done wrong?
What have I done to deserve your wrath?
I thought you said you would be with me to the very end.
Then why has my knees buckled and for food I fend?
What about all those promises that you have made to me?
Were they prophecies or lies embedded in a book of
hypocrisy?
God, where are you?
Don't you see my fears?
Or has your hatred kindled against my tears?
Is it safe to say you don't care anymore?
Or has your love dried up and there simply is no more?
Has your patience grown thin?
Should I wait while you decide?
While I stay on the straight and narrow and avoid the broad
and wide.
Should I linger in darkness waiting to die?
Or will you save me and prove to me you are not a lie?
I'm screaming for you to help me, but you give me your
back instead.
It seems, even you wish I was dead.

Road to Damascus

It is amazing how inept we as humans can be,
Too busy chasing darkened streets, our fleeting happiness
and our own regretful existence and mortality,
To see what God sees when He looks at us.
What is life but a pound of flesh filled with perversions
and lies,
Punctuated by the sweet nothings that permeate the toxic
air we breathe?

We sell our souls for a mere nickel on the dollar.
Unwilling to see past our noses, our children are rendered
helpless by those who lust after innocence.
Too blind to care, our faces become a blank stare,
A canvas unwritten to our inevitable demise.

It's no surprise
Then,
That our women have been relegated to prostitutes and
whores.
Women, pull up your panties and cover your ass,
This life is more than sex and debauchery and more about
class,
Get tutored in the ways of the past when a woman was a
lady no questions asked!

Our men, all creating and perpetuating the same carnal sin,
Creating babies and forsaking their God-given wisdom and
power within.

We blindly seek guidance where there exists none
From those long gone,
Yet we fail to see that those men all pointed to God.
We repeatedly turn our backs on the Creator to embrace
and worship that which He has created,
As though our lives still have no true meaning or
significance.

We fight wars that have no clear identity or purpose, just
so we can exert and abuse our powers,
But He who sits high and looks low will bring retribution to
our doors.

How can we do evil and expect good?
Didn't you know that this life became a book the moment
we were conceived?
Now, what will your pages read,
When you bow down before Him on your knees?

Wake up, my people, to the promises of the past,
When the Almighty God promised us sweet peace at last!
Grasp God and not just the concept of Him!
Grasp God, instead of sin,
Because our God is merciful to the end.
There will come a time, a time when our praises and
prayers will not suffice,
But until then, let's endeavour to remove the motes from
our ever-evil eyes,
So that His wrath will not be kindled upon our heads,
For He who sits high and looks low,
Who makes the heavens His throne, the earth His footstool,

And the clouds mere dust on his feet,
Sits in anger, yet everlasting love, grows impatient at our
lack of peace.

So, be warned; be lovers of God, instead of lovers of sin,
and our legacy will never diminish from our children.
Be like babes, humble and mild,
For this desolate life is but for a little time.

Cry not when we can pray,
My people,
We must change our wicked ways.

For even I have sinned,
Turning my back on the God within,
To foolishly seek after lies and pain,
Seeking that which was never intended for men,
And now my eyes have grown cold with delusions of
grandeur,
While my kingliness is slowly ravished by vultures.

I cried to the Lord who enriches my mouth with words to
prosper;
All those who will listen,
"Men who fall off their horses in the midst of war and get
back up again will be rewarded justly,
But those who lie stiff-necked dressed in apathy and
indifference will be obliterated."

Don't let lies confound you,
Don't let hatred become your accuser in the sight of
Almighty God,

For God is God all unto Himself and is able to be your
refuge and weapons of war.
Be filled with wisdom of those that the prophets of old
foretold,
Those self-appointed prophets and lovers of men who will
seek to erode and corrode the truth of God already
written in stone.
People of God,
The time is at hand, and we must now cement our minds
towards one deliberate goal,
The goal to kill our flesh,
As we retain our eternal souls.

September

In my afflictions, they took much delight,
As they plotted to destroy my reputation and dismantle my might.
But God smiled because He knew better.
For this wasn't my end, but the beginning of a new chapter.

They thought I would have wept and bowed my head in regret,
But I was already forewarned by God of their malicious intent.
They basked in their victory as I fought my way from the deep,
Not knowing that the God I serve neither slumbers nor sleeps.
And as they await my demise with bated breath,
God whispered in my ear, 'Don't worry, cause they ain't seen nothing yet.'

'Let not your troubles define you, but let them refine you,' He said,
Knowing already what troubles lay ahead.
So I put on my coat of amour to pray and prepare,
For the coming hardships that I would now have to bear.
And even though my anger still persisted,
'There is a lesson to be learnt,' He insisted.
So, forget the bad times you had and do remember the good ones,
Because everyone will most certainly have their day under the sun.

Hollow

Ply me with your lies,
So that my ever-consuming soul will wax rich and cold,
Indoctrinate me with your religiosity,
So that I may find a smoother way to hell.
Inundate me with your philosophies,
That I may think myself greater than God.
Feed me with your populace notions,
That the colour of my skin defines my destiny.
But touch not the Lord's anointing,
Touch not my will and purpose,
Touch not the fire that burns within my flesh,
For righteousness and truth,
For I will not become hollowed or hardened.
So go ahead and dismantle my intellect with your might,
Intoxicate me with your false prophecies,
Impale me with your sharpened tongues,
Go and sever my existence from this mortal tomb,
But my stain can never be removed.
For, I was here.

Karma

Karma is the choices that you made yesterday that either
haunts or celebrates your todays
It's the pain or joy you had caused others in so many ways.
It's that woman you married or that man you are about to
divorce,
Its punishment for never feeling any remorse.

It's the pride in your children's eyes or the hatred on their
faces,
It's that quiet accomplishment or that disappointment in all
too familiar places.
It's that hope that God had remembered all of your tears,
For the many hurts you experienced at the hands of
others for all those years.

Karma is that special dream that you had but never lived.
It's that life you could have helped but instead, you chose
not to forgive.
Karma is that deed you did when you thought no one else
was looking.
It's that time bomb to your award or demise that never
stops ticking.

Each day, we give life to Karma, whether good or bad,
Because karma is our actions that can bring forth joy or,
in the end, will make our days sad.
So let us be wise in all our thoughts, conversations, and
actions one to another,

And treat all those we meet like they were our sister or
brother.
Because karma depends on what you do right now,
For this will determine whether your todays will be filled
with happiness
Or
Be filled with bitter tomorrows.

Chapter Three

A Peremptory

An obscure puzzle of a man,
That has many pieces of his animate soul dispersed
throughout the hearts and lives of countless women,
Even he has yet to discover or understand.
So kind are his words,
So flattering is his demeanour,
That you can't be anything but impressed with his innate
confidence.
He teaches,
He loves,
He comforts,
He damages,
Without even realizing the indelible prints,
He has left on minds, hearts, and souls.
He is but a man, after all.
He is pain's and despair's advocate to all women.

Unrequited

He says I'm perfect but not for him,
That my skin is beautiful,
And my loving is as insatiable as sin.
That he loves my legs when they are wrapped around his waist,
That my eyes are like pools of water;
Void of any disgrace.
He whispers sweet lies to ensnare me to do what he pleases,
To hurt me while I'm still on my bended knees.
He touches me with the darkness as I seek the light,
As I become a victim of my own plight.
He smiles at me as he subtly steals the glory from beneath my feet,
Confounded, I succumb to his every need.
My body he loves, but my mind he never mentions,
As I lie crushed beneath his cruel intentions.

My Same

Be careful of him and his exquisite lies,
That masquerades as truth,
Beware of the danger that lies within that forbidden fruit.
Though subtle, his intentions are skewed and a well-disguised
pretence,
He will stop at nothing until he devours your innocence.
He will deceive you into thinking you deserve less than what
you are truly worth,
As his hands fiendishly snake up your skirt.
You then close your eyes and wish him well,
For with that one moment of pleasure, you shall surely tell.
But by then, it would have been too late,
Because you would have been just another victim that was
prepared deliciously for his plate.
With tears in your eyes, you will sorrowfully blame him for
the hurt you feel,
But by then, the damage would have already been done, and
you would have become another spoke in his ever-spinning
wheel.
Now grieved and enraged by his apparent happiness,
You cry because your life has been reduced to an utter
mess.
For in her eyes, you see your mistakes in flesh and bone,
And your heart becomes bitter, and your soul begins to
groan.
Now your child's life is filled with your heartaches and pain,
Now that your mother's mistakes continue with you... again.

Sullen

Touch me with your sullen grace,
Whilst I think it's real,

When inside, I know, I feel that you are not true,
But now, whilst you are in my arms,

Let's pretend that it is.
Let's pretend that you really love me,
And that our love is genuine.

Let's pretend that we are forever destined to be
together,
But when we let go,
Let us not pretend anymore.

Scars

I met the devil once,
And he was everything I ever wanted in a man.
He was everything I thought I needed,
He was full of love for me,
But alas, we weren't meant to be.
His eyes spoke an untold truth,
That I was too afraid to see,
That I wasn't the one he needed at all,
Those truths ultimately lead to my downfall.

He lied,
But am I surprised?
Denial can be so decadently sweet.
Love makes such fools of us.
He left me to juxtapose the pieces of my fragmented
heart,
And as I look at the shards,
A different woman I have become,
Damaged and broken,
To all those that choose to love me,
I am void and stripped of any real human emotions.

But am I surprised?
No, not at all.
For the pain I felt still resonates to this day,
Because the stain of him just won't go away.
So I let it stay to rot and pollute,
Making it impossible for love to grow and produce new
fruit.

And I die daily, unwilling to forgive the hurt he caused,
As I slowly become that woman I never intended to be,
A woman; other than me.

Hurt Me Just a Little Less

Could you hurt me just a little less?
Seeing how much I love you,
Could you not be the monster that you are and try to love
me too?
Could you just hurt me a little less this time?
I wanna make peace with my soul,
Because all this fighting with you is slowly taking its toll.

Could you hurt me just a little less?
Could you not make something so pure become so evil?
Could you just try to see all the pain you have put me
through?
I beg of you.

Speak to me like you did when we first met,
Or is that too much to ask of you these days?
Or,
Have we now gotten to that place?
Where nothing matters anymore.

Give me back that man I once knew,
The man who promised to always be faithful and true,
The man who said he would never hurt me or make me
cry,
The man who was always there and who was always willing
to try.
Because I swear,
I can't keep cleaning up your mess
So please, just try to hurt me just a little less.

Me, Myself, and Him

I have poured gasoline and struck the match,
Ain't no way he is ever coming back.
His face marked a trail to a bruised ego,
My tears blaze a trail toward love and glory,
My life is no longer steeped in misery,
For I am now my own Saviour.
For with his burden, I became weak,
But with his departure, I now stand firmly on my own two
feet.
Because the race isn't for the swift,
But for those who can endure,
That's why his 'do not disturb' sign no longer hangs on my
door.

He thinks that he has left with the better part of me,
But time will reveal that it couldn't be,
Because the part he took was bitter and cold,
Filled with the regrets and pain of an angry soul.
He left the renewed and confident me behind,
The me, which his hatred couldn't find,
The me, who will only get better with time.

You see, love shouldn't hurt at all,
It shouldn't make you feel insignificant or small.
It should make you feel inspired,
It should take you to a higher plane of existence.
Listen to a woman who has been there before,
If it is that your man ain't worth loving anymore.
For if you stay,

A piece of you will die each day,
Until there is nothing left to despise,
So be wise...

Fists Full of Tears

I killed another man today.
I reached into his chest and tore out his beating, bloodied
heart with my bare hands.
It serves him right for loving me, for wanting me.
Don't you know I'm a deliberate poison?
That suffocates, strangles, and kills.
I inoculate, then intoxicate, and ultimately annihilate.
Please don't let my unassuming beauty betray your wisdom.
Because as sure as the sun rises, I will kill you.
I will murder your trust, shit on your respect, butcher
your hopes, and smother your dreams,
Despair is what I have become now, it seems.
I will intrigue you, entice you, and seduce you,
And as your eyes become fixated on my thighs,
And as your lips water for these hips,
My hands slowly hold your life within its deadly grip.
And I will kill you,
I will slowly watch you die,
As you desperately try to understand the reasons why.
I'll watch you try to figure,
How something so lustfully exquisite could be so horribly
bitter.
Much pain I have inflicted and many lives I have destroyed,
But still, all man desire me.
I'm an indiscriminate drug,
Disguised with big tits, a small waist, a firm ass, and alluring
eyes,
I will infect you with my sugar-coated honey drizzled
sweetness,

And then laugh as your life spirals into a magnificent mess.
I'll watch you crumble and stumble into despair,
As I leave you hopeless and broken, crying fists full of tears.

Free

Everything is alright until I close my door at nights,
When the real me comes alive.
I slowly peel away the many untruths I lived today,
I take off my clothes and remove my shoes,
To reveal a body that has been battered, discarded, and
used.
I remove my stockings and bra that whispers the untold
truth,
Of a life that has been damaged repeatedly at the roots.
I slowly remove the makeup, the mask, and with it, the lie
you have come to know,
Of a confident woman, who really is wounded and has lost
herself a long time ago.
The eyeliner, the concealer, the rouge, hide the mental
anguish and abuse,
Only to reveal a broken, bitter, and resentful muse.
The long fake eyelashes hide a pain so rooted and thick,
Much like the painted stain of my favourite lipstick.
The eye shadow that makes my face and eyes glow,
Covers the afflicted hurt buried so deep below.
The flawlessness of my perfect foundation,
Soothes the beast within and quiets the heart-wrenching
condemnation.
The creams, elixirs, and serums I use to make my skin look
more youthful, lighter, and supple,
Conceals the mistakes, the confusion, the emptiness, and
the loneliness that no one or nothing can topple.
The hairpiece I've glued and sewn to my head to make my
hair thicker and longer,

Is brushed aside by the real me, who couldn't be more sombre.
Then the nail polish goes,
And with it, the illusion that I have a perfect life as well as perfect fingers and toes.
Then I stand naked, stripped, bare, raw, and exposed,
Weeping, angry, pained, feeling disposed.
I cry real tears that fall to the ground,
Feeling so ugly and empty, I allow my sorrows to drown.
Until tomorrow, when the sun rises and welcomes a new day,
I wipe my tears, cover the hole in my heart, and put my mask back on and become someone else again today.
Everything is alright until I close my door at nights,
That's when the real me, the true me, comes alive...

Sedative

I need a sedative for my flaws.
Is there no haven from my sins?
It seems my past deeds now haunt my steps throughout
the corridors of life,
An anomaly am I.
One who sits with the opulent,
And hovers among the poor,
No shelter for my head,
Even I now wish I was dead.
Destined for greatness, it's apparent,
But life mocks my haughtiness,
And increases my sorrows,
And still, love eludes me always.

Sorrow is now my friend,
Always there to console and hold my hand.
And as my hair grows grey,
And my presence goes unannounced,
I ruminate on the life lived,
And the hurt I have caused.
I am but a man, sings my unheard cry,
This too is why we live only to die.
And if I thought having love was an attainable goal,
It is only an excuse to look beyond my faults,
While I ignored my soul.
They say: "Love covers a multitude of sins,"
But isn't the real sin, never realizing the God within?
I will now face my woes and blame no one for them,
For what is life, if not a conundrum?

Venom

You say you don't like me; pick a number and join the line
I'm not here to pursue your destiny,
I'm here to fulfil mine.
You say you can't stand me, go ahead, make a statement,
But don't think for a minute, not even a second, that my
life will become as hard as pavement.
You say I'm too feisty, too lippy, and too bold,
Well, I'm sorry for you, truth be told.
You say I'm arrogant, a tad bit rude, and rough around the
edge,
But weren't you the same one who betrayed me and tried
to push me off that ledge.
You say I won't make it without someone like you,
But I got news for you, not only will I make it, but when I
do, you still won't be worth the gum stuck to the bottom
of my shoe.

You say I'm too easy, a bitch and a hoe,
But weren't you the same one who taught me everything I
know.
You would like to believe you are so much better than me,
I not only laugh at that, but I beg to differ, better yet,
disagree.
You preach and pretend to be something you're not,
Then turn around and have the audacity to point your
finger at me and put me on the spot.
You say you won't stop until you discredit and sully my
reputation,

If I were you, I would remember who you are before you
hand out any condemnation.

You say I will never ever be your friend again.
Ha!
Let me not disappoint you, but rather assure you that
before this poem ends, I would have already gained ten.
Don't think for a minute that I haven't heard the venom you
have been spewing behind my back,
Trying to undermine my integrity, but it's too cemented and
too intact.
And just a reminder, in order to break me,
You have got to try much harder than that.
You see, now that I have moved on, I couldn't care less.
Better luck next time in creating another one of your
mess.
And oh, since I have left, I haven't cried, nor will I shed a
single tear,
All that's left to do is to buy a t-shirt with your face on it
that reads: "Hypocrite, Beware!"

Victim

How do I breathe when I'm my own worst enemy?
How do I see when I've become a victim of me?
Speaking tongues and screaming Halleluiah in the open,
As I secretly make lust in the darkness.
Who have I become?
A lie that glistens like pure gold on the outside,
But a sepulchre on the inside, filled with dried white bones
and utter desolation,
I have become like dung on the face of the earth, dried
and baked by the sun until I evolve into nothingness.
Am I an animal?
A dog, which eats its own faeces?
A cradle of lies and utter failure awaits me,
I am exposed.
My insides have spilled onto the ground,
All dangling, like this seductive inferior skin I wear so well.
I walk around with a crooked smile and a roll in my hips,
But I'm an utter lie, a mystery that seeks to be erased.
Let my lies consume me ,
Let my failures ignite me,
Let my truth be told,
I didn't want to be here!
Where is my God when I need Him the most?
Has He left me and gone?
Is He tired of me, of my lies and unfaithfulness, my broken
promises that crumble under His tests?

How do I breathe when I'm my worst enemy?
How do I see when I have become a victim of me?

I'm desperate to find myself lying under these bodies of
men,
Touching, kissing, betraying, using me for their own
gratifications of sin.
As I lie buried beneath them, my pained tears and the
burden of their weight suffocates my very existence,
But still, I lie there stiff-necked and foolish, refusing to
understand what I have done to me.
I have lost,
That woman who I was has long gone,
Perhaps never to return.
Besides, I wouldn't recognize her at all anymore,
The hope in her eyes, the pride of her thighs, the strength
in her back, the curve of her waist, the dip in her hip, the
possessiveness of her voice, the power of her mind have
long, long gone,
Leaving behind this empty husk of herself.
I need time to pray:
Dear God, please rescue me from this barren life of
emptiness, pain, and confusion,
Restore me to my honour and might again,
But God doesn't answer liars and lovers of men.
I am lost and desperately need to be heard,
I need some laying of hands to exorcise these demons in
me, who ravish my soul so effortlessly.
Please Lord, Please Lord, hear my pleas,
Come down and save me from myself before my end
comes so expectedly,
Have mercy on a sinner;
A sinner who loves you but who can't seem to find herself
in spite of you,

Who craves your attention and your embrace,
But who lies hopeless, shamed, and enveloped in disgrace.
How do I breathe when I'm now my own worst enemy?
How do I see when I have now become a victim of me?

Visions of Sin

I lie spent and hopeless on the floor,
As I ponder about the life I have lived before.
I cry as my life spirals out of control,
As a deafening silence slowly creeps deep into the
reassessment of my soul.
My face now stained with wasted tears,
As I succumb to my heartaches and my pain.
God doesn't care, so He just walks away,
Unable to feel the weight of my dismay.
The devil continues to dazzle with his dance and tricks,
While I lie beaten and battered, he continues to kick.
Grey skies and darkness now cling to the room,
As the space I'm in slowly becomes my tomb.
No one will come to save me now,
I don't think they could if they even knew how.
Visions of sin envelope my thoughts,
As I contemplate the reason for my existence and at what
cost my soul was bought.
Forsaken and forgotten have become my truth,
As I search to find what went wrong and why I'm unable to
pluck it from the root.
Gone is my faith; it's now replaced with perfect sadness,
As I am forced into the corner by my conscience.
I try to starve my salacious appetite for sin,
But somehow, it still finds its way back in.
So I lie still and hopeless on the floor,
Unable to heal my life, which has now become this open
sore.

Suicide

As each day passes, a piece of me dies,
Unwilling to reason, I contemplate suicide.
Death begins to cradle my soul like a warm, comforting hand,
As it lovingly wipes the tears from my sullen face.
It embraces me so delicately and so beautifully,
That I succumb to its seductive whispers,
Its kisses tenderly sedate me,
I bow my head in defeat as death slowly becomes me.
Then I impassionedly slit my wrist,
The blood flows so warmly, so perfectly,
Drip, drip, drip, drip, drip, drip.
As each droplet crashes to the floor,
I smile weakly as my thoughts stray to the life I lived,
How hard it was and how easy death is.
My body weakens and falls limp as death creeps in and life forced out,
A single tear rolls from my eye,
Unable to live but I'm willing to die.
My breath now grows hoarse as blood gushes from my severed vein,
No God and no angels come to my rescue as I lay on the cold floor, dying in vain.
Tick, Tock, goes the clock on the wall,
As it counts down the minutes, the seconds that I have to live.
I finally slip into unconsciousness and then into the darkened light,

My eyes close for the last time and nothing matters
anymore.

Chapter Four

Be Kind - For My God

Almighty God be kind to us,
Be abundant in your mercies,
And let your mercies precede your judgments,
Guide our faith and forgive our insolence.
Keep us mindful of our flaws and deficiencies,
But remember us in our strengths,
For every man has been in your presence.
We have all been blessed by your mighty hands,
Created in your awesome image,
Touched by your love and bathed in your infinite
possibilities.

Heavenly Father, when we fail, be patient with us,
Help us not to derail our purpose,
Only to become tufts of grass strewn by the wayside of
life,
Keep us humble in all our human transactions.
For surely it is honourable,
Protect our minds from hatred and impurity,
Give us your love to conquer all our enemies,
While you bless us with your grace to see in them, the
goodness they possess.
What will we do without you Almighty God?
We have nothing to give that is worthy of your
magnificence,
For though trials, hardships, burdens, indifference, and
temptations are all inevitable,
But with you, oh Lord, it is indeed possible for us to
overcome them all.
Amen.

Bloom - For Amoya

Straighten up, grow up, and find yourself,
Free yourself from all those shackles that will endeavour
to bind you to the ground.
Stretch your arms out wide and lose yourself in the
beauty of you,
Exhale, then breathe; let it all out and watch your sorrows
that were mountains all crumble to your feet,
Then smile, brush them aside, and walk away,
Let the air embrace your skin.
Then feel as your spirit blooms and erases the lies that
you were told,
Grasp life's endless possibilities while you allow your fingers
to caress the blessings bestowed.
Learn to creep before you walk,
Learn to listen then think before you talk,
Be aware of the God in you always,
Knowing, having faith that pieces of Him are embedded
inside of you.
Let not your fears become a constant or permanent
companion,
Instead, pray and forgive yourself for the mistakes you
will assuredly make.
And remember that time and love heals every hurt and pain,
And that even your heart will mend again.
Be forever an optimist,
Be steadfast in your own purpose and wisdom,
But be always humble before God,
And He will prosper and direct your path.

Love wisely,
Give willingly,
Pray unceasingly,
Hope constantly,
And your name will never be forgotten,
But will forever be written in stone.

I Know a Woman

I know a woman who gives all she can,
Unlike the self-righteous, indignant rich man,
Who gave only what he thought would pass the test,
This woman gives her life, her all to be the best.

Her love, her kindness, her never-ending care,
In hopes that one day in her Saviour's presence, she will
share,
To stand on that day to hear Him say, without a stutter,
'Oh good and faithful servant, welcome,'
He will proudly utter.

With passion and undying faith in her soul,
The kingdom of Heaven, she will finally behold.
Though life's hardships can be such a burden,
With her strength and faith, she will overcome every
hurdle.

She remains a beacon of light,
Of God's enduring love and might.

This exceptional woman resides with us all,
My sister and my friend, I pray that you will forever stand
tall.

Chapter Five

The God in US

The pastor preaches that when we die,
That hell rejoices and angels cry.
Is this why we live: to suffer, struggle, and serve?
Only to see our children die of a death they don't even
deserve.
And if "God so loved the world that He gave his only
begotten son,"
Why would He then turn around and create that man who
invented the gun?
If God then promised to love us and always be there,
Why, then, is our world filled with so much pain, tyranny,
and despair?
Or if He is the God that sticks closer than a brother and
a friend
Why, then, are we hurting over and over again?
And if He promised to provide our every need,
How come our children we can't even feed?
"For it is a righteous thing for God to recompense
tribulation with great distress to our enemies,"
Yet each day, we decrease as our enemies increase
Where is the God promised by Abraham, Jacob, Isaac, and
Moses?
Has He wandered off somewhere to relax and smell the
roses?
While those who need him so desperately,
Are being persecuted unmercifully.
Where is the God who pronounced that His hands cannot
wax short and that He isn't a man that He should lie?

Has he simply abandoned us to live in a great big mansion in the sky?
Where is the God who said He is our Rock of Gibraltar and our perfect salvation?
Is He more concerned with the devil and not His children's growing frustrations?
What about the God who is the same yesterday, today, and forevermore?
Is it then safe to say that's why the rich get richer and the poor remains poor?

Where is the God that people speak so passionately about?
Is He fast asleep, unable to see our sorrows and unwilling to hear our pleas, or is He too scared to face our desperate shouts?
Where is the God that declared that He is our high brazed wall?
Has He simply neglected us to watch us blindly stumble and fall?

Where is the God to whom the Bible speaks?
The only one who can offer us sweet, perfect peace?
Some say: "Gone are the days when God would fight for us,"
But I believe that God is waiting for us to find the Him in us.

Testify

In the darkness that was my mother's womb,
I testify,
That even before my hands and feet were formed, my
purpose here on earth was already born.
I testify,
Before I even had a smile, much less a face,
My indelible print was marked and could not be erased.
I testify,
Before I had a brain or even a heart,
Almighty God blessed me with tenacity so great
It was unlike any other; I was set apart.
I testify,
Before I had cells, arteries, muscles, or even veins,
My God created in me a greatness that could not be
contained.
I testify,
Before I could move or even lift my head,
God consecrated me with perseverance to overcome any
obstacle, no matter how dread.
I testify,
Before I had fingers or toes,
My God anointed me with incomparable strength to
overcome life's blows.
I testify,
Before I could see, touch, taste, hear, or even smell,
My God had ignited in me a fire to persistently do well.

Now, listen to me my child, He whispered softly in my ear:
"I have encrypted bits and pieces of me in you so that you can take on your journey,
So please do handle with care,
In a world that will seek to destroy and hurt you and hate me,
But always remember who you are and from whence you came,
And know that during your battles, you can forever call upon my name.
I will be there to hold your hand through it all,
Especially, when your troubles have you pressed against life's wall,
And when times get hard, and you may feel like giving up or running away,
Remember, I am with you always."
I testify.

Purpose

If you woke up this morning,
Put your hand over your heart,
Close your eyes,
And really feel it beating.
It's called purpose,
And you are alive for a reason.

Believe in your dreams and they may come true,
But believe in yourself and they most definitely will.

Never get comfortable,
Because there's always room to do better,
Be yourself,
Because there's always things you can do better than
someone else.

You will mess up,
Nobody's perfect,
But don't let a small mistake ruin everything.

Let go of everything that doesn't impact your life
positively,
Because no one else has the power to make your life
good or bad,
Only you.
There are many reasons to say no,
But think about the one reason to say yes,
Because you only fail when you have given up,
On yourself.

Remember that there aren't problems,
Only solutions.
Enjoy moments with those who make you the happiest,
For the best teacher you will ever have in life,
Is experience.

The things you put up with,
Are the things you will most definitely end up with,
So have faith, praise, and thank God in all things,
And your purpose will manifest in everything.

If You Must Cry

If you must cry,
Cry because you are absolutely blessed and highly favoured,
And because all the obstacles and tests that you will encounter today
Will be your accomplishments and testimonies tomorrow.

If you must cry,
Cry because you're happy and not because you are sad,
Cry, because unlike so many others, God has favoured you
to see one more glorious sunrise.

If you must cry,
Cry because you are perfect with all your flaws,
And that God, in all His infinite wisdom and love, made you
uniquely in His own image.

If you must cry,
Cry because, unlike so many, you have friends and family
who genuinely care for you and who will always love you
sincerely.

If you must cry,
Cry because you are wiser today than you have ever been
in spite of it all.

If you must cry,
Cry because your inner beauty is far more precious to
others than that of your outward beauty.

If you must cry,
Cry because as you live, your strengths become pillars of fortitude that surrounds and protects you like the mighty hands of God.

If you must cry,
Cry because, just like the sparrow, God's eyes are lovingly fixated on your yesterdays, your todays, and your forevermores.

If you must cry,
Cry because the God of Heaven would rather die than have you suffer death.

If you must cry,
Cry because your children and your children's children are forever blessed and comforted by the Most High God.

If you must cry,
Cry because God will not forsake you nor allow them that seek to harm you to ever prosper in their deeds.

But most importantly, if you must cry,
Cry out to Almighty God, who is your refuge in times of danger, your peace in the midst of the storm, and your solace in times of great distress.

Infallible

A blessing can be palpable, tangible, or even abstract,
It can be found in the mundane as well as the monumental.

A blessing can be derived from pure pleasure and elation,
It is the embrace of a loved one and the honest smile of a child.

A blessing is a gift that can never be taken away unless we choose to give it up,
It is life, love, and the never-ending pursuit of happiness.

A blessing is acknowledging God in all our hopes, dreams, goals, aspirations, and pursuits,
It is found in the soundness of our minds, the power of our bodies, the love in our hearts, and in the fruits of a woman's womb.

A blessing is the privilege to live, love, and relish life to the fullest,
It is the soft breeze in the morning and the warmness of our nights.

A blessing is not contrite or contrived,
Instead;
Nay,
Rather,
It is the promise that was given in Psalms 23.

A blessing is not merely a slight of hand or a flick of a wrist,
Nay,
Rather,

It is the wisdom of God, His peace that surpasses all man's understanding, God's love that endureth all generations, and His faithfulness to never forsake us.

What Man Meant for Evil

There will be times when life will seem unfair,
When our situations will be too much for us to bear,
When those who we thought were friends,
Will forsake us and won't be there to see us through the
end.
We may feel like turning our backs on the world,
Unable to deal with the pain life has hurled,
But remember that people are people, and we can't change
that,
So don't be persuaded to go toe to toe or tit for tat.
Instead, we should pray and hold strong to what we know,
and let God take care of the rest,
Because He specializes in results and is more than able to
bring us through our tests.

All our trials, burdens, and obstacles are to help set us a
part,
To endow us with wisdom as they strengthen our hearts,
For we often find ourselves in places and circumstances
that we ought not to be,
And He always provides a way for us to clearly see,
That the path that we have now taken wasn't the intended
one,
Somehow, He always finds a way to get us back to His
glorious plan.

This world can be a cold and hard place, and this has been
proven to be true,

But who God loves, He chastens, and that means, He will
always see you through,
For no river is wide enough, no sea is too deep, and no sin
is too great,
For Him to deliver you and bring you back to your
honoured former state.
And although the push and pull of the world may have you
pinned down,
Pray, trust, and have faith that He will pick you up from
off the ground.

Boulders

God will give us boulders to push up a hill,
It isn't for our detriment but rather to strengthen our will,
It is to teach us that the path to righteousness is one less
taken,
But it is the only path we ought to be taking.

God gives us tests that interrupt our seemingly perfect
lives,
But it isn't for us to develop anger or hatred, and it surely
wasn't meant to create strife,
It is to show us that life, with its innumerable hiccups,
delays, and disappointments,
Must never overcome nor interfere with our peace and
contentment.

God allows struggles, heartaches, and pain,
But it's not for His pleasure, and it's certainly not for His
gain.
It is to guide us to the understanding that though life is
flawed,
That it can be made even worse without the help and
wisdom of the Lord.

God gives us Himself each and every day,
His word that He will never deny us no matter how long we
choose to stay away,
So when next you go through a test, a struggle, or you
may have a boulder you must push up a hill,
Look back at where He took you from and know that He
will carry you even farther still.

Lamentations

Though this ship called life will sometimes wade,
Though the many moons of life will inevitably fade,
Though we may gnash our teeth at the thought of that day,
Though our faces will be painted in grief and coloured in shades of grey,
Though mothers will weep for the children they have lost,
And fathers will pound their chests in anguish at the unimaginable cost.
Now that their souls are broken, and no solace can be found,
For their legacy is now buried beneath the ground,
For though our sorrow is now exposed,
And though the end may now seem so very close,
Take heart in the soundness of purpose.

Though our cries and questions may go unanswered and seem to be wasted,
Now that the sting of death we are now faced with,
We can't seem to find God in the unfolding of it all,
But be though humble and listen for His still, silent call.

So be not worried by the hows and the whys,
Be not troubled by our earthly ties,
But instead, let us learn from our own fleeting mortality,
That tomorrow is neither promised to you nor me.

We should then aspire to make today the day in which we extend ourselves,
To those amongst us who are alive and desire our love and help.

For those who were here and are now gone, have given us the chance to make this first powerful step,
Because death, though painful and shattering,
Gives us the opportunity to make amends and to give freely of ourselves... again.

So, take comfort in the Lord's infinite wisdom, promises, peace, and unwavering mercies,
For it is He who giveth and taketh away in its appointed season,
And it is He who truly loves us without a reason.

Not Easily Moved

I will not die tonight,
No, I will not walk gently into the darkened light
I will not bow my head in submission,
No, I will not deviate from my purposed mission.

I will not die today,
I will not allow myself to become a victim of another day,
I will not let my fears overcome my prayers,
I will not let my burdens become my trials.

I will not die tomorrow,
I will not let today's pain become tomorrow's sorrow,
I will not succumb to my disappointments and flaws,
I will not let your words defeat my cause.

I will not die now,
No, not when I've come so far.
I will not die cold and forgotten in the midst of the war,

I will not die,
Today,
Tomorrow,
Or tonight,
Oh no!
I will not die without a hard fought fight!

I WILL NOT DIE!

About the Author

Ceyleena Green grew up in two of the most volatile communities in Kingston, Jamaica. It was in these violent environments that she found solace in writing. She began writing at the tender age of eight years old, as a means of suppressing the despair that she lived in. In her school life, she showed a keen interest in Language Arts and went on to attain a grade one in English Language at the Meadowbrook High School.

While in high school, she fell in love even more with creative writing, which soon allowed her to become a part of The Christian Chronicles as an Editor and Contributor.

She is an up-and-coming poet and author who has already written three books that are to be released shortly. A Preponderance of Thoughts is her first attempt at publishing her works as a poet/author and the first in a series of books that expresses her poetical and writing strengths.

Her influences include a gamut of the literary greats, such as: Langston Hughes, Claude McKay, Maya Angelou, and Edgar Allan Poe. She is also greatly influenced by the writings of the Legendary, Bob Marley, and the Father of the Civil Rights Movement, Marcus Mosiah Garvey.

This author, however, masters and hones her own skills in the art of poetry and storytelling, bringing her own individual blend and eclectic mix to the foreground of the art form.

Tamarind Hill Press
www.tamarindhillpress.co.uk